RAF100
For Children

F.J.BEERLING

Illustrated by
GARETH BOWLER

Copyright UK Ministry of Defence © UK Crown copyright 2018
© Fairyfaye Publications 2018

ISBN: 9781999752057

ISBN: 9781999752057

Poetic licence has been applied on occasion!

Edited by Denise Smith www.dspublishingservices.co.uk

Published by Fairyfaye Publications.
For events and all enquiries email fairyfayepublications@gmail.com

Fairyfaye
Publications
www.fairyfayepublications.co.uk

Book design by Gareth Bowler

Printed in Great Britain

Sopwith Pup

Hoverfly Mk1
Helicopter

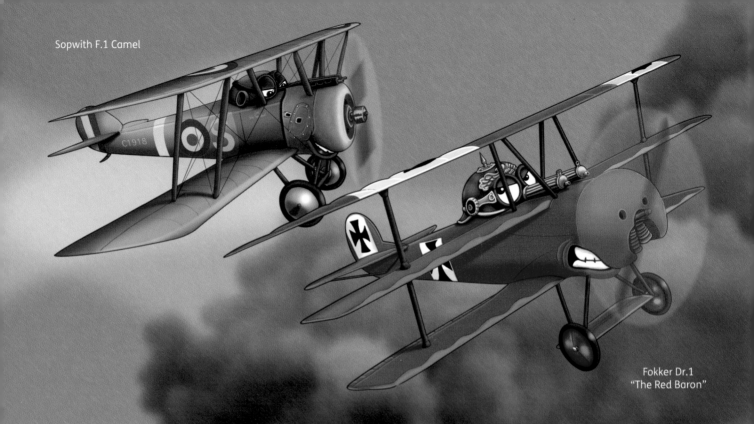

Sopwith F.1 Camel

Fokker Dr.1
"The Red Baron"

Camels?!

Did you know that the Royal Air Force is 100 years old?
It has been one of the most powerful air forces in the world
throughout its 100 year history.

At its largest, the Royal Air Force had over one million
men and women and nearly 55,500 aircraft.

It is the oldest independent air force in the world!

But that's not all;
the Royal Air Force also had a squadron of camels.
Camels!!?

No, not the four-legged kind, these were Sopwith Camels,
single engine bi-planes and the Royal Air Force also had
nine squadrons of bomber planes that they flew
during World War I.

A camel...
not a plane, can't fly
and wasn't part of the
Royal Air Force!

The Royal Air Force

When the British Army's Royal Flying Corps and the Royal Naval Air Service came together on 1st April 1918, the Royal Air Force was created.

Its purpose was to keep our skies safe from the threat of enemy air attack...

...And Lord Trenchard, who was a British Army officer, was known as the Father of the Royal Air Force because he helped establish it, and took command of it in the same year.

He also used some money to help build the Benevolent Fund.

This fund gives help and support to the Royal Air Force staff and their families during times of need, and is still going!

Keeping in touch!

In 1921, the Royal Air Force set up its own weekly postal service...

Vickers Vernon
Troop Carrier

...and that service is still going.
You can send an Aerogramme, or "bluey" as they are called, for free.

A "bluey" is called a "bluey" because it's blue!

Sopwith Cuckoo

Fairey Fawn

Flying Faireys?!

The Royal Air Force flew brilliantly named planes during World War I and the 1920s, such as the Airco de Havilland Bomber, the Sopwith Cuckoo, the Blackburn Dart, and even the Fairey Fawn!

But these aircraft were small, made of wood and canvas and not designed for air attack...

...So in 1924, the Royal Air Force introduced its first all-metal fighter aircraft called the Armstrong Whitworth Siskin III. Longer, stronger and better equipped to defend our skies.

Armstrong Whitworth
Siskin III

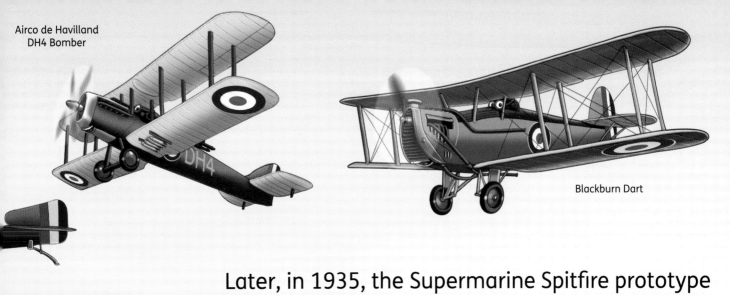

Airco de Havilland
DH4 Bomber

Blackburn Dart

Later, in 1935, the Supermarine Spitfire prototype
took to the skies for the very first time and went on to become
one of the most successful fighter aircraft ever built.

By 1939, ten Spitfire squadrons
were ready to do battle with enemy aircraft
during the Battle of Britain.

Supermarine Spitfire
Prototype

K5054

Battle of Britain

In 1940, at the beginning of World War 2, during the Battle of Britain, many young Royal Air Force fighter pilots lost their lives fighting in the skies above Britain protecting us from enemy invasion...

...And it was their courage and great bravery during that time that led Winston Churchill to give his famous speech:

Hawker
Hurricane Mk.1

Supermarine
Spitfire Mk.1

"Never, in the field of human conflict, was so much owed by so many to so few..."

The Lancaster Bomber
had a crew of seven;
from the pilot to the gunners they
worked hard together as a team,
and flew in many daring missions...
...mostly at night!

de Havilland
DH.98 Mosquito

And although it didn't take part in the Battle of Britain,
along with many other bomber
aircraft, including the Wellington
and the Mosquito, it did help
us to win World War 2.

Vickers
Wellington Bomber

Hawker
Hurricane Mk.II B

Lancaster
Bomber

Helicopters!

When World War 2 ended, in 1945, helicopters became a part of the Royal Air Force.

Royal Air Force Andover was the first helicopter training school and the Hoverfly Mk.1 was the first Royal Air Force helicopter to take to the skies!

Westland WS-61
Sea King

Helicopters are amazing; the Sea King search and rescue has saved people from the sea and rescued them from mountains..

Boeing CH-47 Chinook

The Chinook helicopter has flown soldiers to wherever they are needed around the world...

...And dropped emergency supplies of food and blankets to people all over the world during a crisis.

Red Arrows

In 1964, the world-famous Red Arrows were formed, and each year a new team of nine highly trained elite Royal Air Force pilots fly the Red Arrow jets.

BAE Hawk T1
Red Arrow

Since 1964, they have displayed in more than 56 countries
and performed more than 4,700 times!

And, did you know that the Red Arrows' motto 'Éclat'
is a French word that means 'excellence'.

Breaking Records

As well as protecting our skies, the Royal Air Force has achieved many great things during its first 100 years of service, including the invention of the jet engine by Sir Frank Whittle.

Supermarine S.6B
Racing Seaplane

Before World War 2, the Royal Air Force broke the air speed record and flew long-distance flights from the UK to South Africa and Egypt to Australia in single-engine aircraft.

In 1969, the Royal Air Force won the Transatlantic London-New York race with the Harrier Jump Jet...

Harrier
Jump Jet

...which can take off and land vertically, and landed vertically in central London near St. Pancras Station!

Vulcan Bomber

Typhoon FGR4

Hawker Demon

Celebrating!

The Royal Air Force isn't just aircraft and pilots.
The Royal Air Force is made up of many different jobs such as:
mechanics, engineers, electricians, chefs,
fire fighters, office workers, welders
and many more.

Bristol Bulldog

Sopwith Camel

Airbus
A400M Atlas

The Royal Air Force has come a long way since the early days
of single-engine wood and canvas aircraft
to modern all-metal, fixed-wing aircraft...

...From the invention of radar and wireless communication,
to the invention of the jet engine and to jets that can take off
and land vertically.

BAE Hawk T1
Red Arrow

Hawker
Hurricane Mk.1

So here's to the Royal Air Force!
All the pilots in the air and all the crew
on the ground past and present;
they have worked so hard to keep
the Royal Air Force flying for 100 years.

From the Sopwith Camels and the
flying Faireys to the Red Arrow jets.
With hovering helicopters that
search and rescue...

...To flying into the future with
supersonic jets, refuelling aircraft,
and even a helmet that helps the pilot
to see beneath his jet and all the
way to the ground!

And this is the F-35B Lightning II jet,
the latest jet to enter service
with the Royal Air Force.

F-35B Lightning II

Happy 100th Birthday to the Royal Air Force...

...Chocks away!!

Lancaster
Bomber

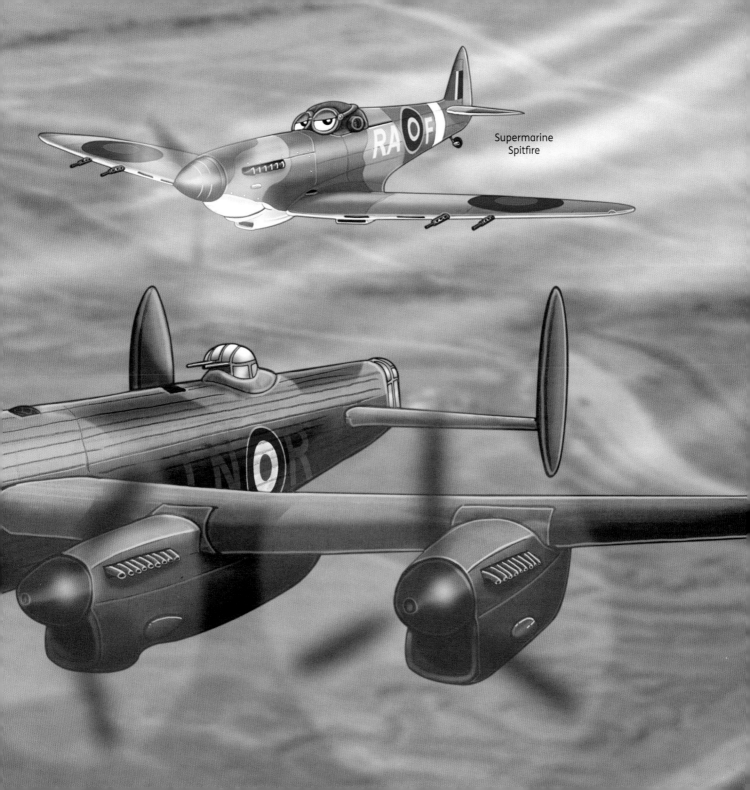

Supermarine
Spitfire

Avro 504K

Sopwith Cub

Westland Wizard